Glitter Glue Fun

Little tubes of glittery fun...add some sparkle to your world!

First published in 2007 by
SpiceBox™
3918 Kitchener St.
Burnaby, BC Canada
www.spicebox.ca

ISBN 10: 1-894722-67-1
ISBN 13: 9-781894-722674

Art Director: Christine Covert
Designer: Morgen Price
Production: Garett Chan
Photographer: James Badger
Editorial Direction: Trisha Pope

Contents

Introduction

Get Ready! Get Set! Go Glitter! There isn't anything that a dab of glitter doesn't make glamorous. Well, perhaps glittering your peanut butter and jelly sandwich might not be a good idea, but almost everything else is great!

This exciting book and kit is sure to inspire you to add a bit of sparkle to your life. Glitter glue is easy to use; whatever fun project you are creating, adding a bit of glitter is sure to turn drab to fab.

In this book there are loads of creative ideas to use your glitter glues with. Many of them are paper projects, but glitter glue also works well on foam, wood, fabric or glass. Use these ideas to inspire your own creativity and have fun glittering!

Points to Remember:

Glitter glue is water-based, which means if you get your glitter project wet, the glue will start to dissolve. So don't use it on clothing or glass that you will need to wash!

Another thing to remember is that you don't want to use your glitter glues on anything that holds food. It isn't safe for eating, and you would not want any food to touch it.

Many of the projects in this book are made with things from around the house, because it is fun to turn your old boring stuff into something glamorous and new! However, don't forget to ask your parents before you glitter up the vase on the side table; it's possible they like it best the way it is. Ask permission before applying glitter glue to items in your house.

Finally, just like any other glue, glitter glue is sticky and can make a mess. So wear your old clothes when working with these glues in case you get some on you, and keep a damp cloth handy to wipe your fingers clean.

Now you are ready to have some fun;

let's go glitter!

Glitter glue and paper get along great!

Use your imagination and some glitter glue to make pretty paper projects that sparkle; the possibilities are endless. On the next few pages, we show you some great ones to start with.

Quick and easy bookmarks and gift tags are always fun to make!

Wrapping Paper

Add pizzazz to plain gift-wrap by highlighting the patterns with glitter glue. You can make a matching gift tag by cutting out a small piece of the pattern and gluing it on craft paper. Punch a hole at the top, add your sparkle and message, and give your gift with style!

You can make your own gift wrap by adding glitter patterns to plain tissue paper or newsprint paper. See how easily glitter glue makes a present extra special?

Don't forget to sparkle the bow!

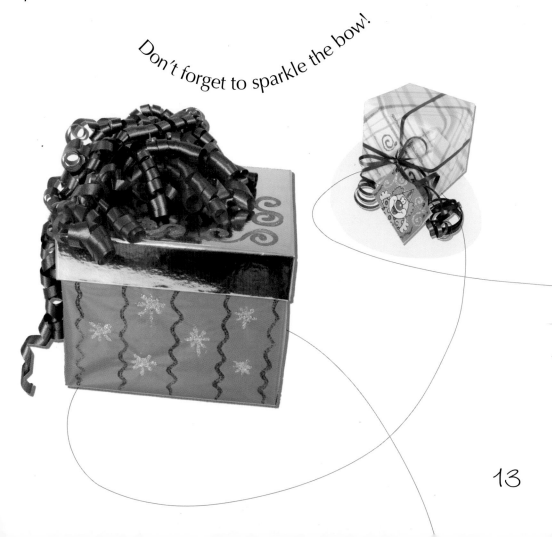

13

Awesome Greeting Cards and Sparkly Stationery

Handmade greeting cards are so popular because they show the recipient that you made an extra effort, just for them!

You can make simple cards out of giftwrap or craft paper or even bits of wall paper! Look around to see what types of paper you can use. Add stickers, ribbons or scrapbook embellishments to dress them up even further.

Hint: Use thicker paper for better results. Thin paper may curl up a bit as your glitter glue dries.

On the left are more creative ideas for sparkly cards using a variety of craft trims. The "Best Friends" card is easy to make using ric-rac from your mom's sewing box. Glue it on the card and trim it with flair using glitter in a contrasting color.

The pink card and the white and silver card are trimmed with a scrap of fabric, ribbon and pretty glitter hearts and swirls — very elegant!

Black is a great background color for glitter glue; experiment with different colors of papers and glues to see which combination you like the best.

Glitter glue adds a wonderful touch to stationery and envelopes as well. Your pals are going to love receiving notes from you in these beautiful cards and envelopes! Use your glue to make fancy borders, create a monogram with your initials and even to underline words in your note for added glam. Who wouldn't love to receive a letter from you on this fantastic stationery?

Add sparkle and glitter to your party invitations — your friends will love them!

17

Fancy Frames

Your glitter kit has paper frames you can use in your room, a magnetic frame for your locker, and photo frame cards to give to your friends. Use your markers and glitter glues to create colorful, unique ways to frame your favorite photos. When you have decorated these and would like to try more, you may want to visit a dollar store. They are a super place for inexpensive, plain frames to decorate. This year, why not create an extra-special gift for your grandparents by sending them your school photo in a frame you decorated yourself?

Hint: Glitter looks especially great on black velvet cards, posters, frames or stickers, and we have included one in your kit for you to try! Use markers to color in the designs first, and then go over them again using glitter glue to make really bold and eye-catching creations.

Light up Your Room!

Customize your kingdom with cool switch plate covers. Ask an adult to help you remove the plastic cover from the wall. Paint it with a coat of craft paint and let it dry, before using your glitter glue (see note below about plastic surfaces) and then decorate the cover with other sparkly embellishments. Ask an adult to screw the plate back into place once dry, and then flick on the switch to a brand new look!

Tip: Glitter glue doesn't adhere well to a smooth or shiny plastic surface once dry. If your frame or any other object you wish to use your glitter glue with is made out of plastic, test your glue on it before creating your design. If the glue doesn't stick once it is dry, you can paint it first with a craft paint and then apply your glue.

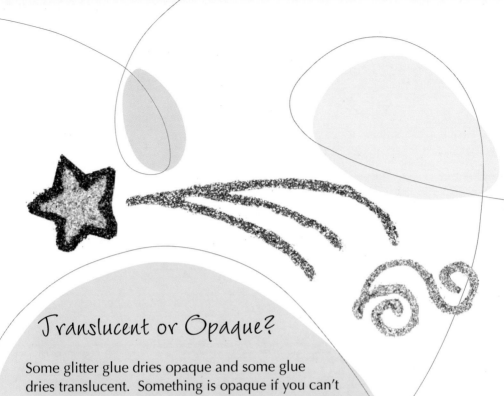

Translucent or Opaque?

Some glitter glue dries opaque and some glue dries translucent. Something is opaque if you can't see through it and translucent is the opposite of this; in other words you will be able to see the paper once the glue dries. Why don't test your glue and see which ones are translucent and which ones are opaque?

When you are using glitter glues that are translucent, the background color that you are using them on will show through. This is good to consider on each project because if you don't want to see the background color, you would choose an opaque glue, or color your design in first with a paint or marker. If you want to see the background color, then choose glitter glue that dries with a more translucent finish.

21

Create designer looks with glitz and sparkle!

Wonderful Wood and Brilliant Boxes

Your local dollar store or your craft supply stores are normally great sources for inexpensive wooden items also that are fun to decorate. Here are a number of cute boxes that each cost only a few dollars, but once decorated look like designer cases.

Let's get out the glitter and start gluing!

23

Glitter your Glass

Sparkly sunglasses certainly make this pretty piggybank look like a star, but we don't recommend you trying this on your own glasses! However, look around your house or go to garage sales one weekend with your folks to pick up treasures made out of glass to decorate. Trinket boxes, vases, candle holders, little dishes; the ideas abound! Just remember, don't try to run anything glass through the dishwasher, get them wet or use them for food; these glittering glass items are for decoration only.

Beautify Your Books

School's in and it is time to take notes, but don't settle for dull notebooks and boring textbooks. Make everything that you write shine with creativity and bring sparkle to your math book with glittery book covers!

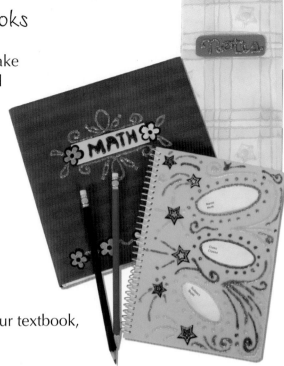

To make a jacket to cover your textbook, follow these simple steps.

1. Fold a large sheet of paper around a closed text book and press it down around all of the edges of your book.
2. Remove the book and open the paper flat. You should have a crease mark in the shape of your open book. Using a ruler, draw a 2 inch (5 cm) border all the way around the crease mark and cut your paper out along this line.
3. Fold the top edge of the paper down along the top crease, and the bottom edge up along the bottom crease.
4. Fold the right and left edges in, along the crease marks as well.
5. Slide your book cover into the sleeves created by the folds, and carefully tape into place.

The best part of covering your textbooks is that when you get tired of one look, you can take the jacket off and design a new one.

Your whole year will sparkle with your creativity!

Funky Foam Fun

Craft foam is tons of fun to use and make creative crafts with. Once your project is put together, be sure to have your tubes of glitter handy to add that extra flair! Whether it is your very own princess tiara, groovy bracelets or a daring dragonfly, you are sure to have a blast with the projects on the next few pages.

Foam shaped bits are fun as embellishments for all your paper projects ... don't forget to add your glitter!

29

Beautiful Bracelets

These funky bracelets are the perfect accessories for any fashion diva. Make one for each of your friends to wear when you have a girl's day out!

Instructions:

1. Use the template A on the right to cut out the bracelet base out of a sheet of craft foam. This will make a bracelet that is 7 inches (18 cm) when on your wrist. You can make it longer or shorter to fit properly, but just be sure to cut the notches in each end as shown so you can fasten it properly.

2. Use template B, C or D to cut out a designer band for the middle of your bracelet, and glue it in place with craft glue. This is optional, you could also use a piece of ribbon, fabric, or a pattern made with your glitter glue.

3. Add the "bling" to your bracelet by glamming it up with glitter, gems, sequins and other sparkly embellishments, and wear your bracelets with style!

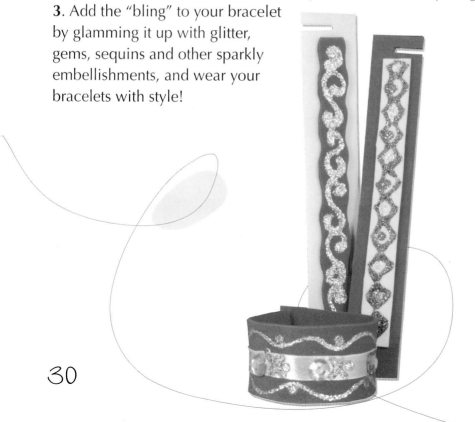

Template:
Trace
at 100%

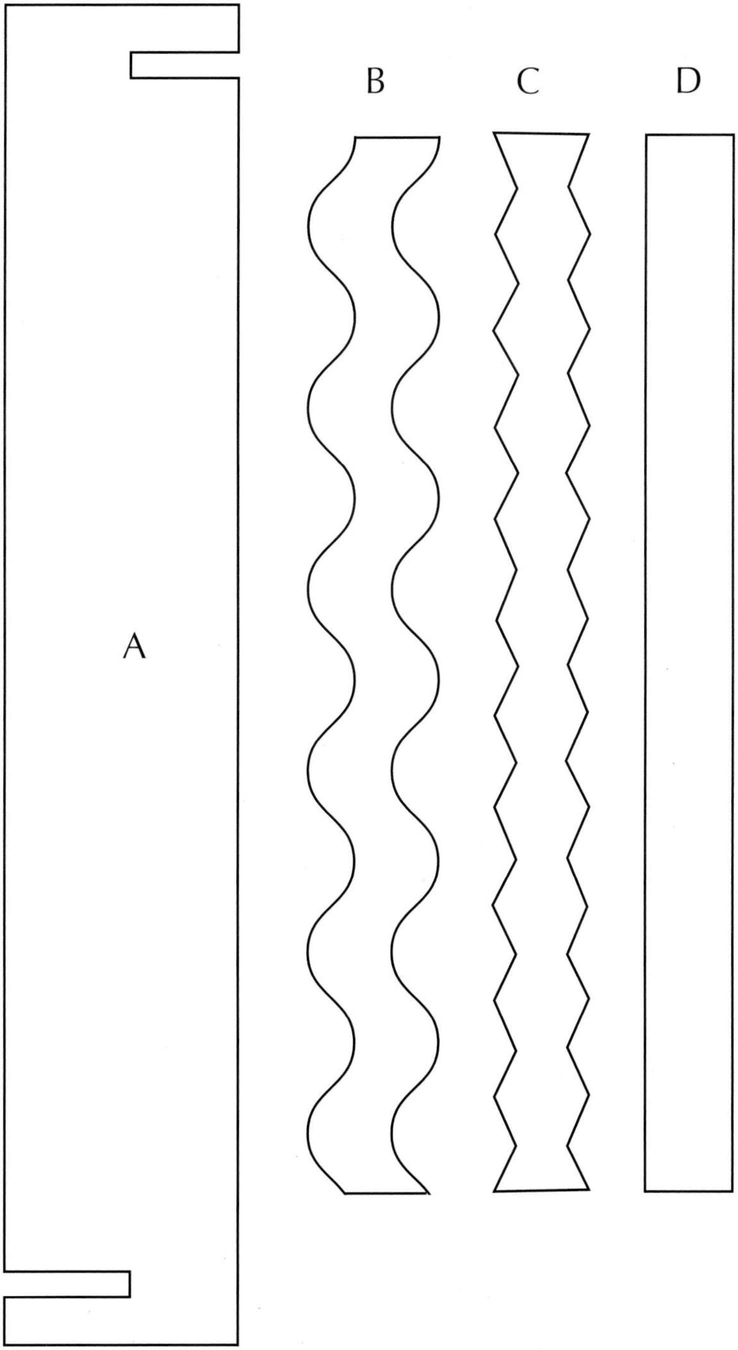

A

B

C

D

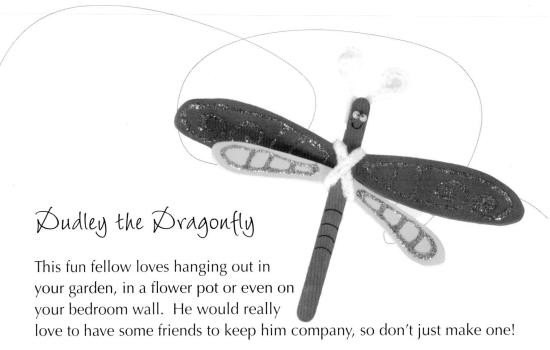

Dudley the Dragonfly

This fun fellow loves hanging out in your garden, in a flower pot or even on your bedroom wall. He would really love to have some friends to keep him company, so don't just make one!

Instructions.

1. Color a craft stick with a marker or craft paint to create the body and let it dry.

2. Trace the two patterns to the right onto craft paper and cut them out. These are your templates. Trace one of each pattern per dragonfly onto a sheet of craft foam and cut them out.

3. Glue the large wing shape onto the craft stick, about an inch from the top. Glue the small wing shape right below it, and let them both dry.

4. Create the antenna by cutting a 4 inch (10 cm) length of chenille stem (pipe cleaner), folding it into a V shape and curling the ends. Glue the antenna to the back of the head.

5. Wrap the remaining piece of chenille stem around the body where it joins the wings and dot a bit of glue to the back to hold it in place.

6. Decorate your dragonfly by adding wiggly eyes to the head or drawing in eyes, a mouth and lines on the body. Then, create spectacular patterns on the wings to make Dudley the Dragonfly shimmer in the sun!

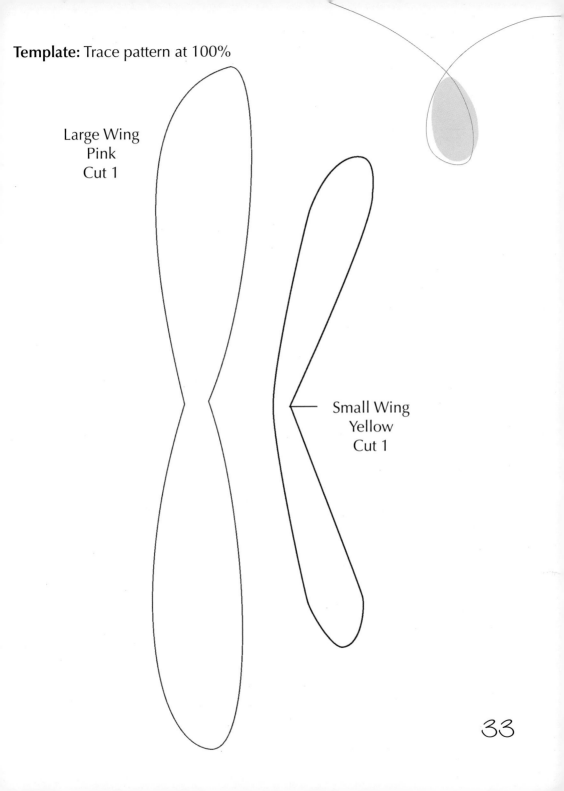

Template: Trace pattern at 100%

Large Wing
Pink
Cut 1

Small Wing
Yellow
Cut 1

33

Princess for A Day

Every princess needs her own crown! These are so fun and easy to make that we recommend you have a matching one for every royal outfit.

Instructions.

1. Photocopy or trace pattern A and pattern B onto two pieces of paper and cut them out to create your template. If you would like a larger crown, then ask an adult to help you enlarge them on a photocopier.
2. Trace each pattern onto craft foam and cut them out
3. Glue the smaller shape onto the larger base piece and let dry completely
4. Once dry, use your glitter glue to decorate your crown so that it is fit for the princess you are! Use gemstones, stickers, feathers, pompoms, or any other fun and sparkly decorations you have.
5. Finally, punch a hole as shown on the template, into each corner of the base of the crown. Cut 2 long pieces of ribbon and tie them through the holes into a bow, leaving one end of the bow quite short, and the other quite long. Now you are able to tie the crown onto your head and you can trim the long piece to the best size for you.

Template: Trace pattern at 100%

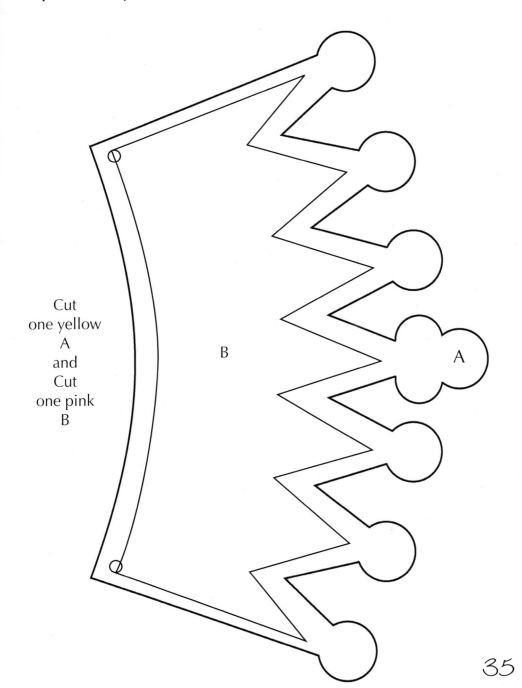

Cut
one yellow
A
and
Cut
one pink
B

B

A

35

Door Hangers

Finally, here is one more fun foamy project to make that is just waiting for a dab of glitter. Door hangers are a great way to personalize the entrance to your domain; warning out unwelcome siblings, or letting people know that you are in!

You can either cut your own shapes out of sheets of craft foam, or buy some shapes precut at a craft shop or dollar store. Here are some ideas for sayings to put on your door hanger:

Keep Out: Danger Zone
The Diva is IN
Princess "your name" Palace
Shh… the Beauty is Sleeping
Girls Only
Quiet!
Smile!

Think of other creative ways to express yourself!

Add glitter glue to ribbons and you got pizzazz!

Glitter Ribbons

Try adding glitter glue to a length of satin ribbon to create a very pretty hair accessory. Or, glitter a ribbon to wrap around a special gift. Tie a sparkly ribbon around your wrist for instant glamour. There are so many ways to use ribbon and glitter, just use your imagination to turn drab to fab!

Final Glamorous Glittery Ideas

Not ready to put away your glitter glue? Take a look around your bedroom, or in the bathroom, the garage, the back yard… you get the idea!

Here are some other items that you can glitter up:

Barrettes and hair bands
Pencil cases and makeup bags
Mirrors, key chains and wallets
Napkins, paper cups and paper chains
Pinwheels and kites
Flower pots and pet rocks
Scrapbook pages
Autograph albums

How many other ideas can you come up with?

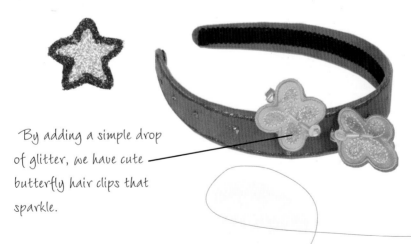

By adding a simple drop of glitter, we have cute butterfly hair clips that sparkle.

Sayings for Your Cards

Here are a few simple messages that you may like to use for the cards you make.

Birthday

Best wishes for a wonderful birthday

It's your special day

Let's party!

May all your wishes come true

Smile! It's your birthday

Birthday

Laugh! This is your present.
Happy Birthday

May today be filled with all
the things you're wishing for.
Happy Birthday!

Friends

Friends forever

If friends were flowers I'd pick you

Or add a silly joke for laughs.

Where does the Easter Bunny go
when he needs a new tail?
To a re-tail store!

How do pigs write?
With a pigpen.

What kind of keys do kids like to carry?
Coo-kies!

What gets wet the more you dry?
A towel!

General

Get well soon

Thank you for always being there

Thinking of you